CELEBRATE YOUR SECOND CHANCE

FINDING YOUR WAY BACK TO SUCCESS

SURESH NATARAJAN & SOWMYA NATARAJAN

Celebrate your second chance

Finding your way back to success

ᐅᐅᐅ

Ms. Jacqueline Sowmya Natarajan

Assistant Professor & Soft Skills Trainer

Communication & Soft Skills Department

KoneruKoneru Lakshmaiah University, Vijayawada campus.

Mr. Suresh Natarajan

Corporate Trainer, Emotional Intelligence coach

NSDC Certified Assessor

ᐅᐅᐅ

This book is dedicated to our parents, who love us

Blessy and Abhi who inspire us

People who stood by us

and to those who are looking for a

second chance to prove themselves.

Contents

Chapter 1

Reflect On The Key Concepts In Chapter 2

Reflect On The Key Concepts In Chapter 3

Chapter 4: Second Chances In Career And Education

Chapter 5: The Power Of A Second Chance In Society

Chapter 6

Preface

Welcome to our book, "Celebrate Your Second Chance: Finding Your Way Back to Success". This book is dedicated to anyone who has faced a setback or failure in life, and is looking for a way to regain their footing and achieve success once again.

Throughout the pages of this book, we will share stories of individuals who have experienced setbacks in their personal and professional lives, but have used their second chance to find their way back to success. We will also provide practical strategies and insights on how you can embrace your second chance and turn it into an opportunity for growth, change, and transformation.

As someone who has personally experienced setbacks and second chances in our own life, we know firsthand the power of perseverance, resilience, and a positive mindset. We wrote this book with the hope of inspiring and motivating others to do the same, and to celebrate their second chance as a gift rather than a burden.

Whether you are looking to start a new career, mend a broken relationship, or simply find more meaning and purpose in your life, this book is designed to help you achieve your goals and find your way back to success.

Thank you for joining us on this journey, and I hope that the stories and insights in this book will inspire you to embrace your own second chance and make the most of every opportunity that comes your way.

Acknowledgements

We acknowledge this book to the following individuals and couples who inspired, guided, and continue to bless our lives through their exemplified living.

1. Mr & Mrs. Augustus
2. President and Sister Solomon
3. President Karl E Nelson, Beverly Nelson
4. President and Sis Bonham
5. Elder & Sis Manwaring
6. Elder & Sis McIntosh
7. Elder & sis Asplunds
8. Elder & Sis Funk
9. Suzzane and Mike Hall
10. Patrick and Maria Cheuk
11. Juswan and Aischa R L Tandiman
12. Brad and Lori Howell
13. Scott & Sherry Wilde
14. Mr. Prasad Rao

ONE
INTRODUCTION

Definition of the term "second chance"

A second chance is an opportunity to make a fresh start or to try again after a failure or setback. It can refer to a specific event or situation, such as a job interview or a relationship, or it can refer to a broader aspect of one's life, such as a career or personal development. A second chance can provide an individual with the opportunity to correct past mistakes, learn from failure, and improve their circumstances. It can also be viewed as a form of redemption, allowing an individual to atone for past wrongs and move forward with a renewed sense of purpose. Overall, a second chance is an opportunity to change the course of one's life and create a better future.

There are several reasons why we should believe in the power of second chances in our lives:

We all make mistakes: No one is perfect and we all make mistakes. Believing in the power of second chances allows us to acknowledge our mistakes and take responsibility for them, rather than dwelling on them and feeling hopeless.

We can learn and grow from our mistakes: A second chance can provide the opportunity to learn from our mistakes and make positive changes in our lives. It gives us the chance to reflect on our actions and figure out how we can do things differently in the future.

It promotes forgiveness: Believing in the power of second chances promotes forgiveness, both for ourselves and for others. It allows us to let go of past grudges and move forward with a positive attitude.

It encourages resilience: Life is full of ups and downs, and believing in second chances can help us to be more resilient when facing challenges. It gives us hope that even when things don't go as planned, we can still come back from it.

It's essential for the society: Second chances are essential for the society as they are the foundation of rehabilitation and promoting the rights of marginalized groups. It helps in reducing recidivism and promoting social justice.

Overall, believing in the power of second chances can help us to live a more fulfilling life. It allows us to embrace change and see failure as a learning opportunity, rather than as an insurmountable obstacle.

The importance of second chances in personal growth and development

Second chances are an important aspect of personal growth and development because they provide individuals with the opportunity to learn from their mistakes, make positive changes, and improve their circumstances.

Learning from mistakes: A second chance allows individuals to reflect on their actions and understand what led to their failure or setback. This can help them to identify areas for improvement and make positive changes in the future.

Overcoming fear of failure: Many people are held back by a fear of failure and the belief that one mistake means the end of their chances. Second chances can help individuals to overcome this fear by showing them that failure is not the end, but rather an opportunity to learn and grow.

Building resilience: Second chances help individuals to develop resilience, which is the ability to bounce back from failure or setback. By accepting and learning from failure, individuals can build the mental toughness to handle future challenges and setbacks.

Promoting self-growth: Second chances help individuals to grow both personally and professionally. It allows individuals to take risks, explore new opportunities, and develop their skills and talents.

Encouraging self-forgiveness: Second chances can help individuals to learn self-forgiveness, which is the process of accepting and forgiving oneself for past mistakes. This can lead to greater self-awareness, self-acceptance, and emotional well-being.

Overall, second chances play a vital role in personal growth and development. They provide individuals with the opportunity to learn from their mistakes, build resilience, and create a better future for themselves.

Are you willing to try the virtue of second chance in your life?

• 3 •

TWO
THE PSYCHOLOGY OF SECOND CHANCES

The psychology of second chances involves understanding the emotional and cognitive processes that come into play when we are given another opportunity to succeed after experiencing failure or setback. It involves exploring the role of forgiveness, self-forgiveness, and self-compassion in promoting resilience and helping individuals overcome the psychological barriers that may prevent them from trying again.

The role of forgiveness and self-forgiveness in second chances

Forgiveness and self-forgiveness play a critical role in the process of second chances. When we experience failure or setback, it is easy to become consumed by negative emotions such as anger, resentment, and guilt. These emotions can hold us back and prevent us from moving forward.

Forgiveness involves letting go of negative feelings towards someone who has wronged us. In the context of second chances, forgiveness may involve forgiving others who have contributed to our failure or setback. By forgiving others, we can release negative emotions and move on.

Self-forgiveness is equally important in the process of second chances. It involves accepting responsibility for our actions and acknowledging that we are human and make mistakes. When we practice self-forgiveness, we can let go of negative self-talk and self-criticism, which can prevent us from trying again. Self-forgiveness allows us to move forward with a growth mindset, rather than being stuck in a negative self-image.

Forgiveness and self-forgiveness are not always easy. It may be difficult to forgive others or to let go of feelings of guilt and shame. However, practicing forgiveness and self-forgiveness can promote resilience and help individuals move past their failures and setbacks.

In addition, forgiveness and self-forgiveness can promote positive relationships with others. When we forgive others, we can strengthen our relationships and build trust. When we practice self-forgiveness, we can develop a stronger sense of self-esteem and self-worth, which can improve our relationships with others.

In summary, forgiveness and self-forgiveness play a crucial role in the process of second chances. By letting go of negative emotions and self-talk, individuals can move forward with a growth mindset and embrace new opportunities for success. Forgiveness and self-forgiveness can also promote positive relationships with others and improve self-esteem and self-worth.

An inspiring story that illustrates the role of forgiveness and self-forgiveness in second chances is the story of **Nelson Mandela.**

Nelson Mandela was a South African anti-apartheid revolutionary, politician, and philanthropist who served as the first black President of South Africa from 1994 to 1999. During his life, Mandela experienced many setbacks and challenges, including being imprisoned for 27 years for his anti-apartheid activism.

Despite his imprisonment, Mandela never gave up on his fight for justice and equality. After he was released from prison, he worked tirelessly to end apartheid and promote reconciliation between black and white South Africans.

Mandela's commitment to forgiveness and self-forgiveness was a critical factor in his success. He famously said, "As I walked out the door toward the gate that would lead to my freedom, I knew if I didn't leave my bitterness and hatred behind, I'd still be in prison." Mandela recognized the importance of forgiveness in moving forward and creating a better future.

Mandela's commitment to forgiveness was also evident in his efforts to reconcile with those who had imprisoned him. He worked with his former jailer to promote reconciliation and forgiveness, demonstrating that forgiveness can promote positive relationships and pave the way for second chances.

In addition, Mandela's commitment to self-forgiveness was a critical factor in his ability to lead and inspire others. Despite the setbacks and failures he experienced, Mandela never lost faith in himself or his ability to make a difference. He practiced self-forgiveness, acknowledging that he was human and that he made mistakes, but also recognizing that he had the power to make a positive impact.

In summary, Nelson Mandela's story is an inspiring example of the role of forgiveness and self-forgiveness in second chances. By practicing forgiveness and self-forgiveness, individuals can move past their failures and setbacks and embrace new opportunities for success. Forgiveness and self-forgiveness can also promote positive relationships with others and improve self-esteem and self-worth.

The impact of past failures on self-esteem and the ability to take risks

Past failures can have a significant impact on an individual's self-esteem and ability to take risks. When we experience failure or setback, it can shake our confidence and make us hesitant to take risks in the future. This fear of failure can prevent us from pursuing our goals and realizing our full potential.

One way that past failures can impact self-esteem is by creating a negative self-image. When we experience failure, it is easy to internalize the negative feedback and develop a belief that we are not good enough or capable of success. This negative self-image can lead to feelings of low self-esteem, which can make it difficult to take risks and try new things.

Past failures can also impact the ability to take risks. When we experience failure, it can create a fear of taking risks and trying new things. We may become hesitant to step outside of our comfort zones, fearing that we will fail again. This fear of failure can be paralyzing and prevent us from pursuing new opportunities.

To overcome the impact of past failures on self-esteem and the ability to take risks, it is important to practice self-compassion and focus on small, achievable goals. Self-compassion involves treating ourselves with kindness and understanding, rather than self-criticism. By practicing self-compassion, we can develop a more positive self-image and improve our self-esteem.

Focusing on small, achievable goals can also help to build confidence and promote risk-taking. By setting small goals and celebrating small successes, we can build momentum and gain the confidence needed to pursue larger goals and take bigger risks.

In summary, past failures can have a significant impact on self-esteem and the ability to take risks. However, by practicing self-compassion and focusing on small, achievable goals, individuals can overcome these barriers and move forward towards success.

An inspiring story that illustrates the impact of past failures on self-esteem and the ability to take risks is that of **Thomas Edison**, one of the greatest inventors of all time.

Thomas Edison experienced many failures in his lifetime. In fact, he is famous for saying, "I have not failed. I've just found 10,000 ways that won't work." One of his most famous inventions, the light bulb, took him over 1,000 attempts to get right. This is a testament to Edison's perseverance and determination in the face of failure.

Despite his many failures, Edison never gave up. He believed in himself and his ability to succeed, even when others doubted him. His self-esteem was not shaken by his failures, but rather fueled by his determination to succeed.

Edison's ability to take risks was also a key factor in his success. He was not afraid to try new things and take risks, even when he knew that failure was a possibility. His willingness to take risks allowed him to discover new technologies and create groundbreaking inventions.

Thomas Edison's story is an inspiring example of how past failures can impact self-esteem and the ability to take risks, but they do not have to define us. Edison's perseverance and determination in the face of failure, and his willingness to take risks, are traits that we can all aspire to. By believing in ourselves and our ability to succeed, and by taking calculated risks, we can overcome our failures and achieve our goals.

Reflect on the key concepts in Chapter 2

By reflecting on these questions and concepts, you can gain a deeper understanding of the psychology of second chances and how it can impact your personal and professional lives.

The role of forgiveness and self-forgiveness in second chances:

a. Think of a time when you were given a second chance by someone. What did you learn from that experience?

a. How does forgiveness play a role in second chances? Why is it important to forgive oneself and others?

c. What are some strategies that you can use to practice self-forgiveness?

The impact of past failures on self-esteem and the ability to take risks:

a. Reflect on a past failure that impacted your self-esteem. How did it affect your ability to take risks in the future?

b. What are some ways that you can overcome the fear of failure and take risks again?

c. How can a second chance help you regain confidence and overcome past failures?

Bringing it all together:

a. Think of a situation where you can apply the principles of forgiveness and self-forgiveness to give someone a second chance.

b. What are some potential risks and benefits of giving someone a second chance? How can you make an informed decision about whether to offer a second chance?

c. How can you use the lessons from this chapter to improve your relationships with others and your own self-esteem?

THREE

SECOND CHANCES IN RELATIONSHIPS

Second chances are not limited to personal or professional achievements. They are also an essential aspect of relationships. In fact, relationships are one of the most common areas where people seek second chances. This chapter will explore the different aspects of second chances in relationships.

The role of second chances in relationships

Second chances play a significant role in relationships as they offer the opportunity to heal and rebuild trust after a significant betrayal or mistake. Giving someone a second chance is an act of forgiveness, and it can be a powerful tool in strengthening relationships.

When we give someone a second chance, we show that we are committed to the relationship and that we believe in the person's ability to change and improve. Second chances can also help us grow and learn from our mistakes, both as individuals and as a couple.

However, it is important to note that second chances are not always appropriate or necessary. Sometimes, the damage done to the relationship is too severe, and it is better to move on. It is up to each person to decide whether or not to give a second chance based on the specific situation and circumstances.

Effective communication is essential when it comes to second chances in relationships. Both partners must be willing to openly and honestly communicate their feelings, needs, and expectations. This communication can be difficult and uncomfortable, but it is necessary for rebuilding trust and working through the issues that led to the need for a second chance.

In conclusion, second chances can play a crucial role in relationships. Forgiveness, growth, and learning from mistakes are all possible outcomes of giving someone a second chance. However, it is important to approach the situation with caution and effective communication to ensure the best possible outcome for the relationship.

There is an inspiring story from India that highlights the power of second chances in relationships. The story is about a young couple, Ravi and Anjali, who had been married for five years but were on the verge of divorce due to constant arguments and misunderstandings.

Ravi had always been insecure about his job and financial status, and his insecurities often led to him lashing out at Anjali. On the other hand, Anjali was tired of the constant fighting and felt like Ravi did not trust or respect her.

One day, Ravi realized that he was on the brink of losing the person he loved the most and decided to seek help. He began attending therapy sessions and working on his insecurities and communication skills. He apologized to Anjali for his past behavior and promised to work on himself and their relationship.

Anjali was initially skeptical but decided to give Ravi a second chance. They started attending couples therapy together and worked on improving their communication and rebuilding trust. Over time, they learned to understand each other's perspectives and needs better, and their relationship became stronger than ever before.

Today, Ravi and Anjali are happily married and credit their second chance with saving their relationship. They have learned that forgiveness and communication are essential in any relationship, and that second chances can lead to growth and stronger bonds between partners.

This story highlights the importance of second chances in relationships and the power of forgiveness and communication. It shows that with the right attitude and effort, it is possible to overcome even the most significant challenges in a relationship and come out stronger on the other side.

The impact of second chances on friendships and family dynamics

Second chances can also have a significant impact on friendships and family dynamics. In both cases, giving someone a second chance can lead to healing, growth, and stronger relationships.

In friendships, second chances can be a powerful tool in overcoming conflicts and misunderstandings. Friends may have disagreements or hurt each other's feelings, but with a second chance, they can work on understanding each other's perspectives and rebuilding trust. It can also be an opportunity to communicate openly and honestly about their needs and expectations in the friendship.

Second chances can also play a crucial role in family dynamics. Family members may have disagreements or conflicts that can lead to tension and strained relationships. Giving someone a second chance can be a way to heal those wounds and work towards a stronger and more supportive family unit. Family members may need to forgive each other for past mistakes and work on communication and understanding to rebuild trust.

However, it is important to note that second chances are not always appropriate or necessary in friendships and family dynamics. Sometimes, the damage done to the relationship is too severe, and it is better to move on. It is up to each person to decide whether or not to give a second chance based on the specific situation and circumstances.

In conclusion, second chances can have a significant impact on friendships and family dynamics. They can lead to healing, growth, and stronger relationships, but they require forgiveness, effective communication, and commitment. It is up to each individual to decide whether or not to give a second chance based on their specific situation and circumstances.

Certainly, here is an inspiring story that showcases the impact of second chances on family dynamics:

The story is about a mother named Maria and her daughter, Emily. When Emily was a teenager, she began to rebel against her mother's rules and expectations. She would skip school, stay out late, and hang out with the wrong crowd. Maria tried to discipline her daughter, but nothing seemed to work, and their relationship became strained.

One day, Emily ran away from home and was gone for several weeks. Maria was devastated and feared for her daughter's safety. When Emily finally returned home, Maria was angry and hurt, but deep down, she still loved her daughter and wanted to help her.

Maria decided to give Emily a second chance, but with certain conditions. She asked Emily to attend therapy, stop hanging out with her bad influences, and work towards rebuilding their relationship. Emily agreed, and over time, they began to heal their relationship.

Through therapy, Emily was able to address her underlying issues and work on her behavior. Maria learned to communicate more effectively with her daughter and understand her perspective. They also began to spend more quality time together, going on hikes, cooking meals, and watching movies.

Today, Maria and Emily have a strong and loving relationship. Emily has grown into a responsible and successful adult, and Maria is proud of the woman she has become. Their second chance led to healing, growth, and a deeper understanding of each other.

This story highlights the impact of second chances on family dynamics. Maria could have given up on Emily and pushed her away, but she chose to give her daughter a second chance. Through therapy, communication, and commitment, they were able to heal their relationship and create a stronger bond. The power of forgiveness and second chances can transform relationships and bring families closer together.

<u>Reflect on the key concepts in Chapter 3</u>

By reflecting on these questions and concepts, you can gain a deeper understanding of the psychology of second chances and how it can impact your personal and professional lives.

The role of second chances in relationships

1. Why are second chances important in relationships?
2. What are some factors to consider when deciding whether to give a second chance in a relationship?
3. How can communication play a role in the success or failure of a second chance?

The impact of second chances on friendships and family dynamics

1. What is the impact of second chances on friendships?
2. What is the impact of second chances on family dynamics?

FOUR

SECOND CHANCES IN CAREER AND EDUCATION

Career advancement and professional development are essential aspects of a fulfilling work life. However, it is common to experience setbacks and failures in one's career journey. In such situations, the opportunity for a second chance can be a valuable asset. This chapter explores the role of second chances in professional development and career advancement.

The role of second chances in professional development and career advancement

The Benefits of Second Chances: Second chances provide individuals with the opportunity to learn from their mistakes and to grow in their skills and abilities. Whether it is the chance to take on a new project or the opportunity to reapply for a job after being turned down, second chances can help individuals regain confidence and demonstrate their potential. Additionally, second chances can provide individuals with the opportunity to explore new career paths and interests that they may not have previously considered.

The Importance of Persistence: In order to take advantage of second chances, individuals must be persistent in their pursuit of career goals. This means taking the initiative to seek out new opportunities and being proactive in addressing weaknesses or areas of improvement. It also means being willing to put in the effort and hard work required to succeed in a given role.

The Role of Networking: Networking can play a crucial role in obtaining second chances in professional development and career advancement. Building strong professional relationships can open up new opportunities and provide individuals with the chance to showcase their skills and abilities. By staying connected with colleagues, attending industry events, and seeking out mentors, individuals can position themselves for future success.

The Importance of a Growth Mindset: A growth mindset is essential for taking advantage of second chances in professional development and career advancement. Individuals who believe that their abilities can be developed through hard work and dedication are more likely to persist in the face of setbacks and failures. They are also more likely to view second chances as opportunities for growth and improvement rather than as a reflection of their abilities.

Conclusion: In conclusion, second chances can be a valuable asset in professional development and career advancement. By providing individuals with the opportunity to learn from their mistakes, explore new interests, and demonstrate their potential, second chances can help individuals achieve their career goals. However, taking advantage of second chances requires persistence, networking, and a growth mindset. With these qualities, individuals can position themselves for success and achieve their career aspirations.

Meet Tim, a man who had a passion for cooking but was unable to pursue it as a career due to financial constraints. Tim had to drop out of high school to work in a factory to support his family, and his dream of becoming a chef seemed like an impossible feat.

However, Tim's passion for cooking never died, and he continued to cook for his family and friends in his free time. One day, Tim's friend recommended him for a job as a dishwasher at a local restaurant. Tim was thrilled at the opportunity and worked hard to prove himself. Within a few months, Tim was promoted to a line cook position and eventually became the head chef at the restaurant.

Tim's dedication, hard work, and passion for cooking paid off, and he was able to achieve his dream of becoming a chef despite facing significant challenges. His second chance at a career in the culinary industry provided him with the opportunity to develop his skills, gain experience, and advance in his career.

Tim's story highlights the importance of second chances in professional development and career advancement. Without the opportunity to work as a dishwasher at the restaurant, Tim may have never been able to pursue his dream of becoming a chef. His second chance provided him with a platform to showcase his skills and eventually become the head chef at the restaurant.

Furthermore, Tim's story also demonstrates the importance of hard work and perseverance in achieving one's career goals. Despite facing numerous obstacles, Tim remained committed to his passion for cooking and worked tirelessly to advance in his career.

In conclusion, Tim's story is an inspiring example of the role that second chances can play in professional development and career advancement. With the right opportunity and a strong work ethic, individuals can overcome challenges and achieve their career aspirations, regardless of their background or financial circumstances.

The impact of second chances on educational opportunities

Education is a critical aspect of personal and professional development, providing individuals with the knowledge and skills necessary to achieve their goals. However, educational opportunities can be limited by various factors, including financial resources, academic performance, and access to resources. Second chances can play an important role in overcoming these barriers and creating new opportunities for educational advancement.

Second chances can provide individuals with the opportunity to continue their education, even if they have experienced setbacks in the past. This can be especially important for individuals who may have struggled academically or who were unable to complete their education due to financial or personal reasons. By providing individuals with the chance to re-enroll in school, access additional resources, or pursue alternative educational pathways, second chances can help individuals achieve their educational goals.

The Role of Support: Support from family, friends, and educational institutions is essential for taking advantage of second chances in education. This support can come in many forms, including financial assistance, emotional encouragement, and academic guidance. By providing individuals with the support they need to overcome educational barriers, support networks can help individuals achieve their full potential.

The Importance of Self-Motivation: While support from others is critical, self-motivation is also essential for taking advantage of second chances in education. Individuals who are motivated to continue their education and who are willing to put in the effort and hard work required to succeed are more likely to achieve their goals. This motivation can be cultivated through a variety of factors, including personal values, long-term goals, and a desire to improve one's skills and knowledge.

The Role of Flexibility: Flexibility is also important when pursuing educational opportunities through second chances. Individuals may need to adjust their schedules, seek out alternative pathways to traditional education, or pursue education on a part-time basis in order to balance other responsibilities. Educational institutions that offer flexible schedules, online learning options, and alternative pathways can help individuals take advantage of second chances in education.

Conclusion: In conclusion, second chances can provide individuals with important opportunities for educational advancement, allowing them to overcome barriers and achieve their goals. However, taking advantage of these opportunities requires support from others, self-motivation, and flexibility. By cultivating these qualities, individuals can overcome educational barriers and achieve their full potential.

An inspiring story that illustrates the impact of second chances on educational opportunities is the story of Roberta, a single mother of two who had always dreamed of earning a college degree but had to drop out of school due to financial constraints. Roberta worked as a receptionist at a local law firm but struggled to make ends meet, let alone save up enough money to go back to school. However, Roberta never lost sight of her dream of earning a college degree.

One day, Roberta heard about a scholarship program that provided funding for single mothers who wanted to go back to school. With the help of her supportive family and friends, Roberta applied for the scholarship and was accepted. Roberta went back to school and earned her college degree in just four years. With her degree, Roberta was able to secure a higher-paying job and provide a better life for herself and her children.

Roberta's story illustrates the impact that second chances can have on educational opportunities. Without the scholarship program, Roberta may never have been able to go back to school and earn her college degree. The program provided Roberta with the financial support she needed to pursue her educational goals and create a better life for herself and her family.

This story also highlights the importance of support from family and friends when taking advantage of second chances in education. Roberta's supportive network played a crucial role in helping her pursue her educational goals and achieve her dreams.

In conclusion, Roberta's story serves as an inspiring example of the impact that second chances can have on educational opportunities. By providing individuals with the support they need to pursue their educational goals, second chances can help individuals overcome barriers and achieve their full potential.

Chapter 4: Second Chances in Career and Education

By reflecting on these questions and concepts, you can gain a deeper understanding of the psychology of second chances and how it can impact your personal and professional lives.

ax. **Identify your career goals:** Write down your career aspirations and goals. This could include the position you want to reach, the industry you want to work in, or the skills you want to develop.

ax. **Reflect on past experiences:** Think about any previous setbacks or failures in your career. Consider what you learned from those experiences and how they can inform your approach to achieving your goals.

ax. **Look for second chances:** Research opportunities to gain experience, develop new skills, or advance in your career. This could include internships, apprenticeships, professional development courses, or networking events.

ax. **Embrace the learning process:** Recognize that second chances often come with a learning curve. Be willing to ask for help, take feedback, and learn from your mistakes.

ax. **Build a support network:** Seek out mentors, peers, or colleagues who can provide guidance and support as you pursue your career goals.

ax. **Stay resilient:** Remember that setbacks and failures are a natural part of the career journey. Stay resilient and focused on your goals, even in the face of obstacles or challenges.

ax. **Celebrate your successes:** Take time to acknowledge and celebrate your accomplishments, no matter how small they may seem. Recognize the progress you've made and the skills you've developed, and use these achievements to propel you forward in your career.

By following these steps, you can implement the concept of second chances in their career and education, opening up new opportunities for growth, development, and advancement.

FIVE

THE POWER OF A SECOND CHANCE IN SOCIETY

The impact of second chances on social inequality and marginalization

The power of a second chance in society is immense. It can provide individuals with the opportunity to turn their lives around, overcome challenges, and become productive members of society.

One of the key aspects of second chances is the ability to provide individuals with support, guidance, and resources they need to succeed. This can include job training, education, counseling, therapy, and peer support. By offering individuals the tools they need to overcome obstacles and build a brighter future, we can help them achieve their full potential and contribute positively to their communities.

Another critical aspect of second chances is the ability to rebuild relationships and trust. Often, individuals who have made mistakes have damaged relationships with family, friends, and loved ones. By providing opportunities for reconciliation, forgiveness, and communication, we can help individuals rebuild these relationships and move forward with a sense of purpose and belonging.

The role of second chances in rehabilitation

Second chances also play a critical role in rehabilitation, particularly in the context of addiction and mental health treatment. Many people who struggle with addiction or mental health issues have experienced trauma, social isolation, and other challenges that can make it difficult for them to lead fulfilling lives.

One of the primary ways that second chances are implemented in rehabilitation is through treatment programs that offer counseling, therapy, and other support services to individuals struggling with addiction or mental health issues. These programs aim to help individuals develop coping mechanisms, address underlying issues, and build a support network that can help them maintain their recovery over the long term.

Another important aspect of second chances in rehabilitation is the role of peer support. Many people who have successfully overcome addiction or mental health issues become peer supporters, offering guidance, mentorship, and accountability to others who are struggling with similar challenges.

Finally, second chances in rehabilitation also involve rebuilding relationships with family and loved ones. Often, addiction and mental health issues can cause strain on these relationships, and rebuilding trust and communication can be a critical aspect of the recovery process.

Overall, second chances are essential in rehabilitation because they provide individuals with the support, guidance, and resources they need to overcome the challenges they face and build a healthier, happier life. Through counseling, therapy, peer support, and family involvement, individuals can develop the skills and resilience they need to maintain their recovery over the long term.

One inspiring story that illustrates the power of second chances in rehabilitation in India is the story of Sindhutai Sapkal. Sapkal was born into a poor family in Maharashtra and was married at the age of 10. She suffered abuse from her husband and in-laws and eventually ran away while pregnant.

Sapkal gave birth to her daughter on the streets and struggled to make ends meet. She began begging for food and money, and eventually started caring for other abandoned children. Over time, Sapkal became known as "Mother of Orphans" and has since dedicated her life to caring for and rehabilitating abandoned and orphaned children.

Despite facing numerous challenges, including poverty, discrimination, and personal tragedy, Sapkal never gave up. She started her own orphanage, the Sanmati Bal Niketan, and has provided a home and education to thousands of children over the years. She has also started vocational training programs for girls, helping them to develop skills and earn a living.

Sapkal's story illustrates the power of second chances in rehabilitation. Despite facing tremendous adversity, she was able to turn her life around and make a positive impact on the lives of others. Through her work with children, Sapkal has provided second chances to those who have been abandoned or neglected, helping them to rebuild their lives and pursue their dreams.

Overall, Sindhutai Sapkal's story is a testament to the transformative power of second chances in rehabilitation. By providing individuals with the support and resources they need to overcome challenges and pursue their goals, we can help them make a positive impact on their communities and the world around them.

The impact of second chances on social inequality and marginalization

The impact of second chances on social inequality and marginalization cannot be overstated. Individuals who have experienced setbacks or made mistakes in their lives may face significant barriers to accessing education, employment, housing, and other opportunities that are essential for their well-being and success. These barriers can perpetuate cycles of poverty, crime, and exclusion, making it difficult for individuals to break out of negative patterns and improve their lives.

Providing second chances can help to break down these barriers and create a more equitable and just society. By offering education and training programs, job opportunities, and housing assistance, individuals who have faced challenges in their lives can access the resources and support they need to overcome their obstacles and achieve their goals.

In addition, second chances can help to reduce the cycle of poverty and crime that often perpetuates social inequality and marginalization. By providing individuals with opportunities to succeed, they are less likely to engage in criminal activity or other negative behaviors that can harm themselves and others. This can lead to a reduction in crime and an overall improvement in community well-being.

Moreover, offering second chances can have a positive impact on mental health and well-being. When individuals feel supported and valued, they are more likely to experience a sense of purpose and belonging, which can improve their overall quality of life.

Overall, providing second chances can play a critical role in promoting social equality and reducing marginalization. By giving individuals the support and resources they need to succeed, society can create a more inclusive and equitable environment for all.

An inspiring story that highlights the impact of second chances on social inequality and marginalization is the story of Bryan Stevenson, a lawyer and social justice advocate who founded the Equal Justice Initiative (EJI) to provide legal representation to prisoners on death row and advocate for criminal justice reform.

Stevenson grew up in a poor, rural community in southern Delaware and experienced racial discrimination and segregation from a young age. He attended college at Eastern University and then law school at Harvard, where he became involved in providing legal representation to prisoners on death row.

After law school, Stevenson moved to Montgomery, Alabama, and founded the EJI to provide legal representation to poor and marginalized individuals who were unfairly treated by the criminal justice system. Through his work at the EJI, Stevenson has successfully appealed the sentences of dozens of prisoners on death row, many of whom were wrongfully convicted or received unfair sentences due to their race or socio-economic status.

Stevenson's story demonstrates the power of second chances in addressing social inequality and marginalization. Despite facing significant obstacles and discrimination in his own life, Stevenson was able to overcome these challenges and use his skills and resources to advocate for others who were facing similar struggles.

Moreover, Stevenson's work at the EJI highlights the impact that second chances can have on individuals who have been unfairly treated by the criminal justice system. By providing legal representation and advocacy, Stevenson and his team at the EJI have helped to reduce the number of wrongful convictions and unfair sentences that have perpetuated social inequality and marginalization.

In conclusion, the story of Bryan Stevenson and the Equal Justice Initiative is an inspiring example of the power of second chances in addressing social inequality and marginalization. Through his work, Stevenson has demonstrated that even in the face of significant obstacles, individuals can use their skills and resources to make a positive impact on society and promote a more equitable and just world.

Chapter 5: The Power of a Second Chance in Society

By reflecting on these questions and concepts, you can gain a deeper understanding of the psychology of second chances and how it can impact your personal and professional lives.

ax. **Volunteering and Mentorship:** Consider volunteering with an organization that provides support and rehabilitation services to those in need. Alternatively, consider becoming a mentor to someone who has faced challenges similar to your own experiences. Share your story and offer guidance and support to help them navigate their own journey.

ax. **Donations and Support:** Consider donating to organizations that support rehabilitation and second chances. This can include monetary donations, donations of time or resources, or simply sharing information about these organizations with others in your community.

ax. **Outreach:** Consider reaching out to organizations in your community that support abandoned or orphaned children, or those that provide support and rehabilitation services to those in need. Offer to volunteer your time or resources to help support their work.

ax. **Empowerment:** Consider ways in which you can empower those in your community who have faced challenges and need a second chance. This may include providing resources or support, offering guidance or mentorship, or simply being a positive role model.

SIX
CONCLUSION

How to take advantage of a second chance when it comes

In life, we all make mistakes and face failures, but what truly matters is how we handle them and learn from them. Sometimes, life gives us a second chance to make things right, and it's up to us to seize the opportunity and make the most of it.

Here are some tips on how to take advantage of a second chance when it comes:

Acknowledge your mistakes: The first step towards taking advantage of a second chance is to acknowledge your mistakes and take responsibility for your actions. This will help you avoid repeating the same mistakes in the future.

Learn from your mistakes: Take time to reflect on what went wrong and identify what you could have done differently. Use this knowledge to make better decisions and avoid similar mistakes in the future.

Stay positive: A positive attitude can help you stay motivated and focused on your goals. Believe in yourself and your abilities, and remember that you have been given a second chance for a reason.

Set realistic goals: Set achievable goals that will help you make progress towards your desired outcome. Break down your goals into smaller, more manageable steps to make them easier to achieve.

Take action: Once you have set your goals, take action towards achieving them. Don't wait for things to happen; make them happen. Be proactive and take control of your life.

Stay committed: Taking advantage of a second chance requires commitment and hard work. Stay focused on your goals, and don't give up when things get tough. Keep pushing forward and stay committed to your path.

In conclusion, I would like to quote Myra Brooks Welch's powerful poem called "The Touch of the Master's Hand". It was first published in 1921 and has since become a beloved and widely recognized piece of poetry.

"The Touch of the Master's Hand" is a poem by Myra Brooks Welch that describes the transformative power of a skilled musician's touch on a battered, old violin. The poem emphasizes the idea that even an object that appears worthless or damaged can be transformed into something beautiful and valuable in the hands of a skilled master.

The poem tells the story of an auctioneer who is auctioning off a battered, old violin. Despite its damaged appearance, the auctioneer attempts to sell it to the highest bidder. However, no one is interested in the instrument, and the auctioneer is about to put it away when an old man steps forward and asks to play it.

The old man takes the violin and begins to play a beautiful melody that captivates everyone in the room. The audience is stunned by the transformation of the battered violin into a beautiful instrument, and the auctioneer realizes that the old man is a master musician who has the ability to bring out the instrument's full potential. The poem ends with the realization that just like the old violin, each of us has the potential to be transformed into something beautiful and valuable in the hands of a skilled Master.

The poem speaks to the idea that even something that appears old, worn, and worthless can be transformed into something beautiful and valuable with the right touch.

'Twas battered and scarred,
And the auctioneer thought it
hardly worth his while
To waste his time on the old violin,
but he held it up with a smile.
"What am I bid, good people", he cried,
"Who starts the bidding for me?"
"One dollar, one dollar, Do I hear two?"
"Two dollars, who makes it three?"
"Three dollars once, three dollars twice, going for three,"
But, No,
From the room far back a gray bearded man
Came forward and picked up the bow,

Then wiping the dust from the old violin
And tightening up the strings,
He played a melody, pure and sweet
As sweet as the angel sings.
The music ceased and the auctioneer
With a voice that was quiet and low,
Said "What now am I bid for this old violin?"
As he held it aloft with its' bow.
"One thousand, one thousand, Do I hear two?"
"Two thousand, Who makes it three?"
"Three thousand once, three thousand twice,
Going and gone", said he.
The audience cheered,
But some of them cried,
"We just don't understand."
"What changed its' worth?"
Swift came the reply.
"The Touch of the Masters Hand."
"And many a man with life out of tune
All battered and bruised with hardship
Is auctioned cheap to a thoughtless crowd
Much like that old violin
A mess of pottage, a glass of wine,
A game and he travels on.
He is going once, he is going twice,
He is going and almost gone.
But the Master comes,
And the foolish crowd never can quite understand,
The worth of a soul and the change that is wrought
By the Touch of the Masters' Hand.
- Myra Brooks Welch

Remember, a second chance is a precious opportunity to learn from your mistakes and make positive changes in your life. Seize the opportunity, stay positive, and stay committed to your goals. With hard work and dedication, you can turn your second chance into a new beginning.

WISHING YOU THE BEST FOR YOUR NEW BEGINNING...

Chapter 1

Are you willing to try the virtue of

second chance in

your life?

Reflect on the key concepts in Chapter 2

By reflecting on these questions and concepts, you can gain a deeper understanding of the psychology of second chances and how it can impact your personal and professional lives.

The role of forgiveness and self-forgiveness in second chances:

a. Think of a time when you were given a second chance by someone. What did you learn from that experience?

a. How does forgiveness play a role in second chances? Why is it important to forgive oneself and others?

a. What are some strategies that you can use to practice self-forgiveness?

The impact of past failures on self-esteem and the ability to take risks:

a. Reflect on a past failure that impacted your self-esteem. How did it affect your ability to take risks in the future?

b. What are some ways that you can overcome the fear of failure and take risks again?

c. How can a second chance help you regain confidence and overcome past failures?

Bringing it all together:

a. Think of a situation where you can apply the principles of forgiveness and self-forgiveness to give someone a second chance.

b. What are some potential risks and benefits of giving someone a second chance? How can you make an informed decision about whether to offer a second chance?

c. How can you use the lessons from this chapter to improve your relationships with others and your own self-esteem?

Reflect on the key concepts in Chapter 3

By reflecting on these questions and concepts, you can gain a deeper understanding of the psychology of second chances and how it can impact your personal and professional lives.

The role of second chances in relationships

1. Why are second chances important in relationships?
2. What are some factors to consider when deciding whether to give a second chance in a relationship?
3. How can communication play a role in the success or failure of a second chance?

The impact of second chances on friendships and family dynamics

1. What is the impact of second chances on friendships?
2. What is the impact of second chances on family dynamics?

Chapter 4: Second Chances in Career and Education

By reflecting on these questions and concepts, you can gain a deeper understanding of the psychology of second chances and how it can impact your personal and professional lives.

ax.   **Identify your career goals:** Write down your career aspirations and goals. This could include the position you want to reach, the industry you want to work in, or the skills you want to develop.

ax.   **Reflect on past experiences:** Think about any previous setbacks or failures in your career. Consider what you learned from those experiences and how they can inform your approach to achieving your goals.

ax.   **Look for second chances:** Research opportunities to gain experience, develop new skills, or advance in your career. This could include internships, apprenticeships, professional development courses, or networking events.

ax.   **Embrace the learning process:** Recognize that second chances often come with a learning curve. Be willing to ask for help, take feedback, and learn from your mistakes.

ax.   **Build a support network:** Seek out mentors, peers, or colleagues who can provide guidance and support as you pursue your career goals.

ax.   **Stay resilient:** Remember that setbacks and failures are a natural part of the career journey. Stay resilient and focused on your goals, even in the face of obstacles or challenges.

ax.   **Celebrate your successes:** Take time to acknowledge and celebrate your accomplishments, no matter how small they may seem. Recognize the progress you've made and the skills you've developed, and use these achievements to propel you forward in your career.

By following these steps, you can implement the concept of second chances in their career and education, opening up new opportunities for growth, development, and advancement.

Chapter 5: The Power of a Second Chance in Society

By reflecting on these questions and concepts, you can gain a deeper understanding of the psychology of second chances and how it can impact your personal and professional lives.

ax. **Volunteering and Mentorship:** Consider volunteering with an organization that provides support and rehabilitation services to those in need. Alternatively, consider becoming a mentor to someone who has faced challenges similar to your own experiences. Share your story and offer guidance and support to help them navigate their own journey.

ax. **Donations and Support:** Consider donating to organizations that support rehabilitation and second chances. This can include monetary donations, donations of time or resources, or simply sharing information about these organizations with others in your community.

ax. **Outreach:** Consider reaching out to organizations in your community that support abandoned or orphaned children, or those that provide support and rehabilitation services to those in need. Offer to volunteer your time or resources to help support their work.

ax. **Empowerment:** Consider ways in which you can empower those in your community who have faced challenges and need a second chance. This may include providing resources or support, offering guidance or mentorship, or simply being a positive role model.

Chapter 6

"

WISHING YOU THE BEST FOR Y

OUR NEW BEGINNING..."